The Five and Dime Store of Eternity

Sean Lause

"The wandering earth herself may be
Only a sudden flaming word,
In clanging space a moment heard,
Troubling the endless reverie."

W.B. Yeats, "The Song of the Happy Shepherd"

Acknowledgments

I would like to thank Tom Beery and Will Wells for their priceless help in revising and editing these poems.

Poems in *The Five and Dime Store of Eternity* have appeared in the following journals:

Inheritance: *Main Channel Voices, Eclectica Magazine, The Innisfree Poetry Journal, Sheila-Na-Gig Online*

I knew a world once deeply in its wounds: *Roanoke Review*

The night I forgot to be afraid: *The New Writer, California Quarterly*

Walls: *Valparaiso Poetry Review*

Dead giveaway: *Chiron Review, The Manhattan Review*

The waiting: *Freefall, Rio: A Journal of the Arts*

Her nightgowns: *Poet's Expresso Review*

Last mirror in the house: *Chest Journal, Third Wednesday Magazine*

Safety manuals: *The Manhattan Review*

How the shadow ended consequence: *Freshwater*

Evangelical haircut: *Jewish Currents*

Samaritan House Samsara: *Samsara*

The old man in the cage: *The Sandy River Review*

Second Semester Hesiod: *Whistling Shade*

The knife sharpener: *Down in the Dirt Magazine*

The wolf as original dreamer: *Caveat Lector, Illumen, The Mother Earth International Journal, The King's English*

Exodus of angels: *The Comstock Review*

My mother's voice in whispers: *Poet's Expresso Review*

Contents

Inheritance

In the back of my grandmother's antique store,
I overhear my grandfather's chanting:
"I don't want to die. I'm afraid to die,"
and my grandmother soothes him, "I know, I know."
And she opens opens doors, drapes, blinds and windows,
old glass lights in carillion colors,
and still he cries his fear of dying.
But I am five and the watches are asleep.
Clocks line the walls, each hushed at a separate hour.
This store is a theater of light,
crystal air, tobacco scents, and hard-bound
books, clasped in secret knowledge.
And now her hands guide me to the garden,
and I am all lit crystal and sun,
as the world rehearses another day.
The light stings like shattered glass,
and broken strings are blowing in the trees.

Brother Snow

Winter 1963
winds berserking into ghosts
reluctantly haunting the air, as if
afraid of their own memories.
Brother we build our separate forts,
yours for war, mine to bind us.
You sculpt parapets high as rockets.
I dig deep round and round,
circling all your walls.
Spitting in my palms, I press and smooth
till that tunnel's as pure as a red bird's song.
You line your heights with severed skulls.
I dig like a white hungry mole.
Finally I'm finished
molding this boundary and embrace,
but when I crawl to you in laughter
you are gone.
Something stole you from me,
some storm beyond my carvings.
Somewhere in that loving circle,
you wandered into time.
Come back now, don't remain
forever locked in the cold and dark.
Brother my love,
why did you melt into Spring?
There is nothing to fear now.
I swear the ring I made for you was peace.

Benediction

Father,
I watched as you shook
droplets of shaving cream
down on my head
from your golden blade,
and we both laughed,
your cracked mirror half-hiding you,
shirt half-undone, muscles clenched like fists.
The day the dog bit my lip
and I cried my doom, but no blood, you said.
I stacked plastic bricks to your ceiling,
built a circular wall all around me,
as if what were hidden could be saved,
as if there were no wars outside
to thunder them down.
The day you came through the back door, shaken,
strangely shrunken inside your huge coat,
one paw of the blizzard swirling behind you,
you searched me out behind the parapet
as you said The Barber had toppled
down his front stairs… I had to look.
He had fallen down, cracked his crown.
It looked like striped candy.
You called the ambulance but it was too late.
But for now you laughed,
and I laughed, as you
flicked snow droplets
down on my waiting face.
I was hungry with smiles as you
laughed to the two of you
deep in that mirror, my heart.

Nachiketa's Quest

See how it was.
One morning, my father
gave me to death.
By noon,
I had entered the snail.
This snail alone
knew how to traverse
the knots in my heart
with unseen worlds.
Deep in my heart
I saw a lighthouse
rise from a sea of blood,
and before it was a door.
To open the door,
I dreamed I was a key.
The door opened into
the prison of my father's pain.
By opening the door,
I set his suffering free.
Then Death said:
"This is Atonement."
The key was my heart.
I stepped through the door,
and through the fire of sorrow,
and found I was a man.
A name touched me
and I was Nachiketa,
the seeker. Deep below,
all wars tumbled to oblivion.

Nachiketa is a hero in the Upanishads. His father gives cows that no longer give milk as a sacrifice to the gods, supposedly to show his piety. Questioning this action, Nachiketa asks his father to sacrifice something of value. He asks his father, "Would you give me away?" In anger, his father replies, "I give you onto Death."

Nachiketa journeys on a quest to meet Death. Death recognizes him as a truth-seeker and offers him three gifts. Nachiketa asks for atonement with his father, to learn the fire sacrifice, and the answer to the question, "What happens to us after death?" Death grants the first two wishes but begs Nachiketa not to pursue the third question. He says the path to salvation is a "razor's edge," painful and difficult. Instead, he offers Nachiketa kingdoms and armies. However, Nachiketa insists on an answer to his question. Death answers Nachketa's question. The seeker will transcend the cycle of life and death and be reborn in heaven only if he overcomes selfishness and learns to see himself in all living things. Nachiketa accepts his answer and is blessed with immortal life.

I knew a world once deeply in its wounds

A candle, a sail, a vigil,
I kept the hours gently and well.
Honey bees festooned the breeze,
and I was the strength and faith of days.
Then one morning, I blindly waved a wand
of dandelion seeds. They tumbled down a wind,
drunken, each suddenly lost, alone,
and time awoke, wound up the sun.
The air gasped like a smothered candle.
Treetops grasped at fleeing angels.
Something came accusing the rose,
and the afternoon sighed with butterflies.
I plunged deep in the trees and gardens
and pulled out webs and roots of wounds.
Everything bled tears or dreams or words,
and the cricket's call shivered through the stars.
I followed a child's cry and found it was my own.
Still, I remember how that final sparrow
sank deep within November winds.

Civil Defense, 1960

Eyes contracted to the dark
watch us from deep lenses,
keeping time and power. Blind.
Hands burrow us into the earth,
pointing us where to cringe and hide.

        We

        are

        here

        waiting

        for

        the

        missiles

        to climb

        their pride

        of nowhere

        then fall, as

        they must,

        through the

        endless

        murder

Yet we dream the electric silence of the stars
that might still guide us, lamp by lamp,
to other worlds of possibility.
And still this world endures in blue,
and still the trees imagine into green.

The night I forgot to be afraid

My father, true philosopher,
refused to build a bomb shelter,
1962,
even though the factory where he worked
had a contract
and wanted him to build one.
Instead, we sat on the front porch swing
and ate ice cream bars
that wept down our shirts
as we listened to intricate crickets
design the dark.
"We'll be all right," he said,
as our deathless feet moved over the lilacs.

Walls

My father guides
the power saw blade
like a skilled surgeon,
while I hold the wall panel
steady, steady, its edges
nearly at my eyes.
The air is dazzled with sawdust
that floats, swirls, then pollinates
my father's crew cut. I picture
poppies blooming there,
unfolding dreams. My fingers
tingle a thrill through my bones.
My father says nothing,
as silent as his bones
that build his strength.
The sawdust scent is sweet.
His hands are big as hunger.
The house stands up wall by wall
and glistens in the sun. Walls nailed
tight to protect and hide. At night,
deep in sleep, my body still hums
to that distant, bitter blade

Astronaut of dreams

Times I returned speechless,
all my words burned up in re-entry,
tumbling through eternities of blue,
learning to speak the silence of the stars.
Once I nearly drowned in timeless night,
dark as the heart of a burrowing beetle,
needles clicking like radioactive crickets,
yet I learned all that light can sing.
Harmonious recess—I left the mother ship
like human popcorn on a string,
guided by moons, luck, and wary angels.
Heaven's jukebox above me spinning dimes.
I threaded planets so distant lonely
they cried like graveyards for a visitor.
When my radio died I sang away
my terror with the music of the spheres.
Time warps changed me to alien, lizard, ape,
lawnmower, butterfly angel and toppled king.
Once I returned with my hair frosted white,
eyes like black holes speaking infinity.
A cardboard box on a summer lawn,
my launch pad and landing—1966.
Guided home by love and fireflies
as constant as any orbit.
While high, high in the distant somewhere,
the moon, like the face of an old man
peering through a curtain, lit the sky
with an ancient longing for return.

Dead giveaway

It was all too good—
the bullet-proof chest,
the x-ray vision,
the super mind, super body,
super legs, thighs,
er, uh…
So the bastards gave him blue hair,
dead giveaway,
like radioactive Brylcreem,
harmatia in pulp,
his secret identity
all unraveled—anyone could see.
But they did not see—not even nosy Lois Lane.
The not-faster-than-a-speeding-bullet world
went Jimmy Olsening on,
scoopless. He stood out—freak—
like green Kryptonite in a valentine—
yet still no one figured it out.
Only language knew, home of
Mr. Mxyzptlk. Magic letters
framed him in inky loneliness,
month after Clark Kent month.
Only words could read his alien longing
that made flight an endless falling.
The earth far below a distant green
rock hurled mightily through silent space,
its only mission—Die Like Spring—
as he must die—
immortally, over and over—
each time he dreams of home.

One way to remember

I can remember ending time
so briefly,
at the top of the highest swing,
wordless, breathless wondering
the sky from old to starstruck,
suspended from the moon,
wind winging me round, upside-down
searching for satellites strung from the stars,
while far below in the darkening green
fireflies lit the night with sudden suns.
And now—hold your breath—and leap—free!
and for an eternal moment
you float weightless in mid-air,
an acrobat of time,
and then you fall through a mother's call
the long way fall to home.
Trust this secret the grass keeps:
The return is the best part of all,
guides you back whenever you wish
from here, to now, to paradise.

Stay with me

Last night she seemed all right,
the gentle German shepherd,
then not well, then seizures,
her hind legs bent numb,
then fear, for the first time,
fear in her eyes that hated
no one, fear that senses death
creeping through the woods.
She calmed only when I
held her huge head in my lap
and stroked her ears all night,
my legs long gone numb
from the weight of her dying.
At dawn her eyes closed,
dreaming of moons,
as if to say—Stay with me,
I stay with you.

The waiting

I never minded Mrs. Dolorez,
who limped across the trailer lot
next door, each day at 1:26,
her crutch creaking like an old tree limb,
her left leg swinging rhythmic as a noose.
She knew her mailbox would be empty.
She had lost both her sons to wars,
and she made this daily ritual
a protest against blood and silence.
But the others…
Their lives were like the silence
between drops of rain.
The tired men and worn-out women,
hands pocketed or touching stray hairs into place,
gazing past each other or down at the gravel,
each day more patiently than the last,
a faith I could never touch
cupped in their palms
as they watched the mailman's hand
drop it all in the wrong slots,
a quick-fleeting purity
denied them.
They spoke or weather,
searched the sky for portents,
then turned back to their separate paths,
speaking gently to themselves,
looking forward to haircuts, hairstylings,
though they must have known that what is cut
cannot suffice,

and that the mailman is sure,
and forgiving,
but never kind or merciful.

Three days to free

It is such a cruel, casual world,
the nuns told me.
It will betray you as it betrayed Him.
It is to be feared and forgiven,
this life on fire with sin.
Yet as I leave the Sunday School,
I release my hands from the handlebars
and—I'm riding in perfect balance!
My arms out wide as wonder,
and the wind can't contain my breaths.
I'll let this wind guide me home
as I pump hard, harder,
gasping with joy and do I dare—
dare close my eyes to all this evil?
Done! I'm riding blind and free.
I can feel the leaf shadows
pierce my body and release it to the sun,
and I guess this world will do
for now, where I am home
wherever the wind blows.
Is this what it felt like for you
on that third day,
when the stone gave way,
and the angel said:
"Come now. It's time"?

The Good War

1
A severed tongue
speaks in silence.
Split the atom
and the soul follows.
Words shattered
to coins
spent for nothing.
Autumn leaves pulse with secret blood.

2
Soldier One
read comic books,
saved his mind by pretending
a force-field around himself
protected him from anything.
But now the magic won't work anymore,
and he hears no one,
and no one hears him.

3
Soldier Two,
poker chair tilted on his back porch wall,
whiskey at his feet,
shoots at doves with his Remington 223
while a puddle at his feet
grows to a stream, then a raging river
that surrounds him and drowns his dreams.

4

Soldier Three is normal,
very, very normal
and safe, shops at Safe-Way,
arrives home each weeknight
at 5:25, when his wife pours
him into a richly-earned martini.
By seven his body is pure grain alcohol
and he stares at the television screen
that glows like Martian cancer
and recites mass casualties from somewhere.
His kids are somewhere, and his wife
is a clenched face sobbing in a pillow.

5

Soldier Four has lots of fun
directing traffic, he's half-blind,
yelling at strangers and
pushing plate glass windows
down on Main Street
from the empty hardware store.

6

Soldier Five learned to swallow his shadow,
with his fear, and all around him he saw
everything feed and feed and feed.
He could stand in a crowd and no one saw him
because his shadow was gone.
And since he was invisible,
he could cry all he wanted,
and set stoplights on fire,
or watch tarantulas crawl from the clouds.

7
Soldier six was an artist of wounds,
carved like cult symbols around his body.
He'd helped liberate Buchenwald.
The mounds of dirt he'd found there
were actually ground human bone,
and the stacks of wood
turned into stacks of children,
all products of German method,
a method he learned, and used,
the day he stuffed his doors and windows,
and blew his house back to origins.

8
Soldier Seven sat in a booth for years
at Frisch's Big Boy,
drinking coffee and talking to himself,
not to himself, I learned, but
to all of us, who were not listening.
He was a flame-thrower
on Iwo Jima,
(average combat life-span four minutes)
Somehow he survived,
but his eyes turned inward,
and the words poured out.
For two weeks he set people on fire,
and then his mind became the fire,
that burned without being consumed.
And now I sit here in his booth,
telling the story.
And I will not let go.

Bees of Autumn

The pears hang
heavy as your eyelids,
the sun distrustful,
an untossed coin.
The long grass yields to unwinding winds,
and the fields are strewn with castaway twigs
that crisscross in snowflake patterns
scattering as we walk.
Your yellow skirt
folds and unfolds
like my grandmother's memories,
the sun coldly touching your shoulder
like a forgiven lover,
as we approach the pear trees
tended by the bees.
The silver dandelions tickle our feet.
Wrenched from the clinging earth,
they give their stars to the sky.
I linger as you pull away,
turning, spinning, waving your arms
free.
You pull the drooping branches
surrendered to your heart.
Embracings call me, softly reaching,
garlanding your shoulders.
The tree arms move with your arms.
The pears nod, tumble, roll,
scarred yellow and brown
into my grateful hands.

I roll onto my back,
spin a pear to reveal
a secret cave.
In shadow,
the heavy honey bees cling,
wings down,
burrowing, heads bowed in reverence,
mouths reaching and reaching,
wings humming contentment.
They depart, finally,
to find others,
land fatly, roll themselves in,
to cling and burrow,
cling and burrow and cling
relentlessly,
as the pears come rolling,
breaking apart,
freed at last
to be destroyed from within.
So must our hearts break,
must fall, break open,
scatter light,
release bees of flight and fall.
Your heart must break
to bind a broken world.
You laugh and say, "Shhhhhhhhhh…"
Still, I remember
your smile of sly revealings,
and bees of Autumn.

Before the contract

The factories encircled us,
like gleaming battleships
with many wars to feed.
I watched my father wear down
from work, a sweat-stained heart
bleeding through his shirt.
By day the workers
dreamed of sleep, the bed
a balm for weary bones.
By night the workers
dreamed of work, their astral
bodies fitting parts to machines.
Sometimes, late at night,
they walked among the shadows of leaves,
seeking the solace of wounded stars.
I know now the world will not end,
because it turns on the endless labor
of those too tired to die.
I did not know this in my
heart, my bones, before
I signed my first bottom line.
What did I know, in my summer
dreams, reading Thomas Wolfe
on my father's front porch swing,
of all these mortal angels
looking homeward for a sign?

Steel enthymeme

Summer job, Westinghouse, sixteen,
I thought I could leap the moon's crippled hand.
Silenced the clock, 4:30 a.m.
screwed two reflector lights on my fender,
cats' eyes of green and blue,
then peddled into the dark
incense of wet leaves,
cold June mist touching my hair
like the fingers of a blind old woman.
Metcalf Street Bridge
cats-cradling the moon,
bending cold to steel—
I stopped at the top for breath,
watched the ball-turret factory dawn,
surveying my new kingdom,
head bowed proudly like a knighted pawn.
I heard sudden thunder,
felt a moon growing on my back,
then brakes like a falcon's cry…
A cold hand touched my bare throat.
"I could have killed you, killed you!"
He held in my face a melon fist
as he sang, "Could have killed you,
stupid kid, nothing but a kid."
He ran to the bridge railing,
said "Forty years I've slaved
in this Hell, forty years for what?"
Below us,
yellow boxcars slatted to Western lands.

He pointed and said "I should hop one of those
and ride away somewhere, anywhere but here."
I nodded to affirm that somewhere,
there might be no factories, no bridges
of steel moons, no stupid kids to kill.

His car was blind as he pulled out,
pounded across the bridge, over the steel scars,
and disappeared in smoke.
I should have been killed, would have been killed,
but something reckless or wise stopped him in time.
All that remained was an apocalypse
the size of a plastic hat,
while my mind, cut and pulsating,
held the unstrung remainder of his memory.

After the hourglass

There is an old stone
near the graveyard,
exiled for inefficiency,
peering blindly toward the wall,
and half-obscured in dusty grass.
Here you lay me down,
and press your breath to mine,
and the beast of all hunger
kneels beneath the moon,
and time is your hair undone to stormy skies.

Why marriage is a reasonable insanity

I'm so nervous I appear at the altar
in white suit and Chuck Taylor Classics.
The minister spots my heathen shoes,
and forgets his Pauline lines.
Down the aisle someone's ancient uncle
squeezes my hand, leers, and says:
"The key is don't be nervous."
I'm nervous.
Your five-year-old niece blinds us
with handfuls of rice at the door.
I back my used car into a new car,
severing "Just Married" to "Just."
A knock at the motel door must be the waiter.
Christ! It's your mother!
She hands me flowers you left behind.
I smile and try not to faint.
I take a swim to work up stamina,
slam my head into the shallow end wall
and float for a minute like a dead fish
knocked to the surface with dynamite.
But all is well, the center holds
most of the night, and the next morning
truckers toot their horns at you
as you stretch out in your sky-blue swimsuit.

Her nightgowns

Her gold reveals the mind's impoverishment
next to the body's guiding contours,
her slink and lace more delicate, more sure
than any man's naked computations.
Her black gown shimmers possibilities,
for what covers, reveals, the way darkness
shivers the stars awake, and mystery
depends on the clues that hide and seek.
Her white is not what you're thinking,
no virgin snows or angel wings for her.
White helps her dream of waterspouts
that guide the waves to summer rain.
Purple is the color of her breakdown
from mourning,
when returning night and silk of love
prove the holiness of tears.
When she whirls in her green
she comes, she comes imagining
old dead Winter to yearning Spring,
and still she keeps a secret of her name.
In blue she triumphs all the male,
for blue subdues him, tames his wars,
turns his baboon soul to Darwin,
and haunts his nights with moons that dream of dawn.

Alone and together

I bolt upright in bed, God don't kill me.
I feel my daggered mind twisting to a cry.
The silence ignores me but you say
Sean, don't worry it's all right, I'm
here no one wants to kill you, and
you hold my thrashing till it stills,
and the invisible enemy is gone
for now, shhhhhh, no one will kill you
while I'm here, but love, I whisper
inside, something wants to kill you,
and will.
I have Night Terrors, you have M.S.
I choke my food in public,
you sometimes vomit yours.
We're quite the night-out-to-dinner pair.
We're both incurable cases,
and time won't let us alone.
Perhaps there's nothing to explain.
The world we fear and dare together
is simply there. Yet tonight let us
stay the darkness, keep despair
from climbing the nearest window.
Let planets ripen to songs of compassion.
They're too calm for me, they're yours alone,
like the celestial birds that float through your eyes,
and guide us back to home.

The lover of Winter

I once knew a woman
who plucked flowers from the moon,
who showed me Winter rains
that never long for Summer.
She pressed my hand
to the wafer of her cheek.
She taught me to run
till my breaths came like stallions.
Then she lay me in fallen angels,
and traced my body from shadow to bird,
touching my veins with songs of icicles
while the snow swirled ballerinas in the sun.
All the treetops
withheld their withered hands.
Ponds amazed themselves to diamonds
while beneath our white quilt,
I slept my first unhaunted dreams.
When she came
I was no longer afraid,
and when she left
I awoke with a big house inside me,
fully-lit,
and a child on a jeweled horse
wondering out the window at the stars.

Last mirror in the house

Death comes, sometimes,
like a merry-go-round,
turning with just the drum
thrumming one-one-one,
with a single lonely rider
round and round, on the same
hysterical horse winding round,
the same lonely rider staring
at you, only you, with
one finger pressed to his lips.
But more often than not
there's free admission,
and death is only
that stupid bald guy
with the scales and
a face like a closed fist,
trying like all sweaty hell
to guess your weight
as it goes down and down
like cotton candy.
But always there is the funhouse,
that is never any fun, riddled
with mirrors and minotaurs,
as you watch yourself turning
into stranger after stranger,
head on the ceiling, hands on the floor,
and you cannot make yourself believe
the whispers behind that last mirror
that reflects what it cannot see.

Words are things

I am haunted by the death in things,
their heaviness, texture, inertia,
the muffled weeping of old shoes in the closet...
And words, too, are things,
after the illusion,
words that hide behind clothes and names,
and bleed, suffer, and are crucified
in dictionaries.
And what, if after all,
death itself is not eternal,
but embodied in dust and stones,
baptized in tears of hornets,
and all hope of resurrection
swaying gently
on a pile of shattered eyeglasses?
Merciless geometry!
Heartlessness in the depths of forms!
I think God is a poem
like Auschwitz,
aesthetic, unified, and cold,
the work death made free,
His masterpiece,
strung with sinews of barbed irony,
and the obscenity of gleaming prosthetics.

The Wounded Bow

Can art ever heal a wounded soul?
It's a question worth asking,
though questions can be blades,
and Van Gogh's crows left without an answer.
We know a leaping yellow cow.
Some have even claimed to see one.
But the price of leaping is the fall,
and most falls don't know where they're going.
Can you heal a wound by entering it?
Every catharsis knows how to lie.
The wounded surgeon knows what I mean:
Everyone dies without a why.
The bow knows the wound is its own taut string,
and its victim's fate wound in the womb.
When disease and cure are one and the same,
Sonny's Blues mean freedom and doom.

Safety manuals

Safety manuals are written in blood.
We turn their pages
by plucking severed fingers of authors
whose wisdom lies in violation, not rules.
It might be safer
to simply buy a gun,
but that will have a safety manual too,
composed by some headless hunter.
The priests are bad enough,
with their relentless purity,
a ferret stuck in their pants,
longing for unoriginal sin.
But the historians are worse.
Who else glues their heads on backwards
on purpose, and enforces penalties
after the game is over?
But worst of all are those
who use no rules at all,
believing themselves original.
They destroy everything but words.

The sigh at the after-forty physical

Down this road goes a three-legged dog,
sensing tumors in trees and bones,
sniffing for my entrails.
I diagnose the dust as I sweep,
sweep it down to stone.
The sun embraced my wife,
planting wounds like gentle flowers
up and down her body
that blossomed into death and poems.
We are conspiracies of flesh and bone.
What we don't know blows out the lights.
I see incinerations strolling the streets,
hear the night weave the winds to ghosts.
The visionary marrow of my bones
screams. What is knowledge
but a graduation of loss
the catalectic mind cannot cohere?
Every crime imagines its detective.
So stretch me on your napkin crucifix,
Doctor, and conjugate my soul.
Even the fly who navigates my arm
penetrates to truth. Can you hear
the spiders clicking through my veins?
Doctor you're a poet of prognosis,
but can you ever see yourself seeing?
Slowly our legs will sprout big clumsy spoons
that catch, and bump, and trip over
the brutal bric-a-brac of this world.
Till the day we step from bed and just keep falling.

What things say when they fade

The poem hears
what it cannot repeat.
The night
absorbs the heron's cry,
a white blade
defying the blind angels.
The owl speaks the moon,
silver cry sewn into black,
longing for what its blind side dreams.
A fact dies
weeping anomalies,
the night, ripe cherry,
hides within the heart.
A cicada shell
waits patiently
on my grandmother's tombstone.
Do the final words of things
dream of shadowless butterflies?
A worm beneath the oak root
digs into the mystery.

How the shadow ended consequence

I know now he was my enemy all along,
although he claimed to be my friend at first,
leaped at my victories, shrugged at my defeats,
circling me whole with the sun.
Then one day he started arriving home
ahead of me, sprawling in my chair
with my cigar already lit, a good book open,
playing a chess match where black moves first.
I have memorized his faith in darkness,
chanted it desperately to aching dawns.
We shot through sanity and daylight
like Dillinger through a two-stoplight town.
Shadows commit no crimes. The little
sticky bastards only follow orders.
Even when they murder they smooth and glide,
shrouding eyewitnesses in ink.
Shadows squat in skyscraper board rooms,
or turn the hidden cogs of secret murder,
and when they grow bored with the sun's decrees,
they make the moon walk bloody through the trees.

The small darkness

A small darkness will not let me go.
Not even tears can wash away its filth.
When night leaves, it remains behind,
watching me, crouched in the corner, swallow-
ing my light, waiting for me to speak to it,
to call it by name, render it my own.
Yet if I speak to it, it shivers its rage.
Even a whisper and it begins to grow
terrified, possibly violent, yet arrogant,
claims it invented the dark, and insists it
knows every song of the abyss by heart.
It follows me room to room, in the corner
of my eye, blocks doors if I try to leave.
It is forever calling for food and water
though as shadow, it cannot eat or drink.
By day it tries to absorb the light.
By night I hear it weeping in the walls.
I must choose—live with it or die.
It's not going anywhere, patient as
Christ's return. I dislike the way it
repeats my name, as if dead echoes
could change the meaning of silence.
How does it speak without a mouth?
Must I wear its sadness like a cloak?
It hates my real shadow most of all.
It wriggles and riddles and writhes, jealous
of that part of me that clings to earth and light,
my true darkness, molded from the sun.
In letters of blood I write each dawn.
I promise it day by day…

Evangelical haircut

He snips and buzzes and shapes me
and tells me, "God has a plan
for each and every one of us."
I say nothing. I never argue
with a man with a plan and scissors.
He tells me, "Adam was meant
to bite that apple." That ripe knowledge.
"No Fall, no Christ." Snip, snip.
"No Christ, no crucifix, no crucifix, no
Resurrection, no Resurrection, no
Salvation for me." Buzz, buzz.
"Think about it."
I'm thinking.
"What's the worst thing
that ever happened to you?"
The mirror. Is that me?
"My wife's death."
I'd rather talk sports.
"God's plan. God sends no
suffering we cannot handle.
No door, there's a window."
It wasn't my suffering.
"What about the Jews?"
"What about them?"
"No Holocaust, no Israel."
"God's plan?"
"You're learning!"

He brisks the cuttings free with a
hand broom, whisks away my angel
cover, beams at his creation.
"See?   Perfect."
I nod, pay him, tip him,
and leave, feeling light,
and free, and alone.

Samaritan House Samsara

Time is counted note by note
in this house where all are abandoned,
only the darkness vigilant,
It interrogates your skin like needles,
while nuns doze like dark-winged doves.
If you should visit Sam's House,
be of good cheer, nervous savior,
It's Optimist Club Baseball Day,
all is well, so sleep in your sound suburbs
that never dream or remember.
Mary, I sense her eyes through the screen.
Her mother sold her for a pop of drugs,
child sex-slave, christened "Nevada Moon."
Bankers had her, evangelicals mauled her.
A tattoo with horns is burned into her palm.
Her kids, Blaze and Cody, tell the story
on our way to Synergy Field,
how their father tried to kill them all
with a sawed-off shotgun. Silently,
I deny it, I just cannot accept it.
When we arrive, Blaze tries to leap
into the Ohio River for the Hell of it.
I buy them peanuts and pennants
with my pleased and plump billfold.
The shotgun, it turns out, was real.
Baseballs and seagulls, dust and angels,
I like this home of lines and rules,
where time takes its time.
I look down and Cody's gone.

Wild Bill's on a tear somewhere,
one day to do this and he's doing it.
My binoculars locate his red pennant
flicking its snake tongue thirty exits away.
He clutches a baseball, a hot dog, t-shirt, and God's change.

On the way back, they slow time down
by counting telephone poles and cattle.
Leaf shadows tremble in awe of Mary,
but she is too frightened to respond.
Rocking, she says only: "In the Fall, the wind bleeds."
The nun tells me with a snicker
how Mary ran from room to room,
crying for her children the whole time,
her two brave sons, first time gone.
Now she holds them in a way I never could.
Mary's tears are smooth and silent
sand pouring from a broken hourglass.
The boys keep saying "When you come again…"
As I ease my car up the neon highway,
all the signs say shotgun, shotgun, shotgun…

Ellipsis

They said she had cancer. People did.
That's all. They whispered it like a scandal.
My wife had just died. My emptiness had pockets.
We were in the Optimist Club together.
She called me up one Sunday.
Would I pick up
her paper for her
at the local Mini-Mart?
Sure.
I delivered her paper.
She taught Spanish at the high school.
Did. Until. Then.
We sat and talked.
She asked if I'd like a cigarette.
Declined. Politely. It's bad for…
We both admired her figure
of Don Quixote on horseback.
Silence. His lance so bent and worn.
She smoked. The weather was fine.
I hate myself. Sometimes I don't.
I was Sancho Panza,
tending the world of shaving basins.
She was Don Quixote,
wanting so much more.
Is the world
golden helmet or shaving basin?
Perhaps both?
A golden shaving basin.
I doubt she ever knew for sure.

The old man in the cage

It is Sunday. The old man in the cage
is wheeled through town again.
His lips tremble with violations.
There must have been a time when he was young.
He signatures the wind with words
they cannot decipher. He is no one.
Though some say he knows when time will end.
His face is a map of sins and visions.
They toss him mirrors and laughter.
He shows them rage and the seat of his pants.
He is the sum of all their ages,
guilty of crimes he can't remember.
At sunset they return him to his cave,
where he'll remain till they need him again
to preen their jaded dream of being gods.

Enter Tiresias, led by a boy

Cries, he cries he is cursed to see the truth,
all of truth, in all of time. But the old man
sees nothing.
His eyes are broken cicada shells.
It was I alone who told him
the gods were displeased, sacrifice denied,
the very earth offended with a death.
I am the guide of the guide.
I know nothing of Oedipus,
except he too was king
once, then he too went blind.
The old seer rages, shakes his woven cane
and cries: "May the gods curse
these arrogant leaders, who plague us
with wars and prisons, men caged
like beasts, children torn from their mother's
arms, and all the dead unburied."
Whispering in his ear, I lead him
down his lonely path.
I am gentle and patient as a star.
He says the stars are falling through his mind.
I will lead him where his birds gather song.

Second Semester Hesiod

Death invented life
to calm its troubled nerves.
The sea invented the embrace of sands
to find its long way home.
The cloud invented the eye
so it could watch itself wander.
The tree invented the ear
so it could hear itself sigh.
The river invented lips
to taste the wonder of thirst.
Silence invented the word
so it would no longer be alone.
The mind invented the body
so it could feel its poetry breathe.
The soul invented passion
to bind itself to the real.

River of masks

My mother's hand rubs
the curving cream
deep into my father's blistered skin.
He spends too much time in the sun,
weaving his garden to Spring.
He sits draped over a chair
like a discarded Venetian Blind,
as she massages aches,
his open sores,
his patient wounds of time.
He stiffens and comes to life.
His eyes seek her out.
He places his hand on hers
and rubs with her.
Finally, he says:
"I don't understand.
Why am I not at work?"
The factory closed twenty years ago.
"I can't be late for work.
Where is my lunchbox?"
Gone.
For a month she tried the truth.
You don't need to work anymore.
It's done. You're all right.
But none of that was real.
So now she tells him:
It's Christmas.
You'll be back at work tomorrow.
He nods.

Does he remember his childhood
Christmases in the Depression,
when he, and so many, got nothing?

He shakes his head as the mystery returns.
He almost speaks, then grows silent.
She continues her daily journey around
and around his beaten body,
fingers quivering with what touch remembers,
loving and longing, healing, healing.
It is a river of masks
they abandon with a touch,
the beauty of a withered hand
no more reconciled to innocence.

Time's Necessity

Eternity can never fathom itself,
knows its depths only through the waters,
finds itself only in the sun-lit web
of the dragonfly's wings,
sees in the dark with the help
of fireflies suturing the night,
touches death only in the tree's golden leavings,
and heaven in the green flesh of Spring.
The lightning's skeleton
guides it through a storm.
The aching bones of the wind
bend it to earth and sky.
A broken cicada shell
frees it to rebirth,
and without a human voice,
it would live forever without a why.
The mortal poem of breath and blood
speaks it to the mystery.
Lovers clutch it, palm to palm,
and press its seeds to the welcome earth.
There it grows and spreads to light,
and grace all-yielding weaves the grasses wild,
the ever-vibrant, endless holy
imagined body of this world.

A veteran playing chess

His fingers quiver on a move.
Then his hand becomes a gentle swan,
gliding down its ebony reflection.
His silence, his sweet cunning, still the
shadow that never seems to leave him,
his dark ghost a memory in silhouette.
Tumbling maple seeds whir with his thoughts.
He sees moves and moves ahead, Prometheus
of pawns, moves with the purity of spheres.
The buildings loom like silent nightmares,
but he ignores their moon-cold shadows.
The board stays calm in black and white.
His son, apprentice, watches, waits, learns
through logic and risk. He knows each move
hovers over an abyss of loss.
Here all rules are clear, and warriors
forever return, and as his son lays down his king,
he knows his father will live on and on.

Fired from McDonald's

Under the golden arches,
she shivers, exiled and alone.
She was not fast enough
for the quick-draw public
whose hunger was a desperate showdown
and whose interchangeable demands
got confused in her young mind.
She always falls to pieces when someone yells.
And they yelled, and the boss yelled, and pointed,
and she saw herself trapped in the eyes of others,
she who was always accepted, simply for being young,
she who is now rejected, simply for being young.
She walks tentatively, at first,
like a blind dove down a church gargoyle.
But then, deep within her breaths,
something takes her over, the resistless rosin
of the sun, polishing its longing bows.
And now she whirls and dances round and free,
joy's sunlight shaken down a sieve.
The sunflowers gaze in delirium
as she pulls a cape of a sudden wind
around her, The Queen of Invisibility.

Math Final

Two men enter a bank.
Each man recognizes the other
as the father of his best friend
from childhood.
Pleasantries are exchanged, then
compliments, based on delusion.
The clock above them both
points to the vault and the exit.
Upon leaving the bank, each man
separately realizes the other
was actually his best friend
from childhood.
Question:
What equals time times time
divided by delusion, subtracting youth,
adding fear, pity, and the Empty Set {   }?
Answer: Laughter for the sake of sanity.

The secret book-sniffer

Hidden in the public library,
I sit encaved in an antique chair
(hand-carved, hand-polished)
in the Rabbi Dorfman Memorial
Reading Lounge, invisible to the
click-clicking multitude, each in his
boxed-in-solitude called computer.
I hold *The Collected Poems of W.B. Yeats*,
Definitive Edition, with the author's final
revisions, all his visions, embraced
in one volume, like the light
around a lunar sphere. I smooth my palms
over its gold initials: *WYB*
He who raged against old age.
Then, with a peek to ensure all is
secrecy, I hold the book close and
riffle the pages to capture the
sweet scent of old print, old pages,
sure binding, craftsmanship that
will never implode like its
weak, paperback descendants.
I inhale with all the desperate passion
of a cocaine addict. Now let them hear
or see! What do they know of textures,
scents, tactile memories, hidden boy-
hood treehouse readings, who only
float in a cyberspace of door-less keys?
Fergus rules the brazen cars!
This is my tower. This is my testament.

I stand with Rabbi Dorfman forever,
in all his lonely, proud desertion.
Against the quick and easy we keep guard,
defending our emblems of adversity,
and the joys of a physical world.

An old woman awaiting a dawn

I awake to dull pain.
Something passed by in the night,
some old miracle, perhaps,
rattled my window, whispered through the corn,
waited sadly for my light, then retreated
down the road with the fireflies
blown by the coming storm.
At dawn there remain only
signature of leaves,
penumbral memories,
whistled tune,
kaleidoscope sky,
an old woman watching through the glass
laughing children linking circles in the grass.
I will lie on the river bank,
my white feet poked in the blue grass,
moon above me, crickets below.
I am not a river, a stone, or star,
and nothing that never dies.
Seek me in nothing strange or far.
Hold me like a child dreaming through your eyes.

And it opens

She turns the key in the grandfather clock,
and turns back the stars in their fates.
Her hair is silver in the doubloon moon
as wars unwind to innocence.
She turns the key again near dawn,
and unlocks time to passion.
Her hair turns black, her pain undone,
she steps into the fury of the light.
Night again, she returns the key,
and time turns back to fallings.
The stars redream the world, all,
sun to moon to dragonfly shadow.
She feels her life ache through her bones
in her bed of love gone and near.
Feet clenched in palms, she curls to a moon,
and sleeps into her memory.

The knife sharpener

A sharp blade's edge
will sing vibration like a word
under the sway of her steady hands,
within whose grasp
such ancient learning lives.
She whistles, presses the pedal
as if playing an ancient organ.
The wheel and the earth turn
to her song of metal on stone,
and birds become the voices of the trees.
She guides the knife in her reflection
until sparks overflow the wind.
The sun's blaze refines to a purity
down the cool edge of blue steel,
and the zodiac turns its menagerie of fate.
She strops the blade to a fine shine,
checks the edge shape with a careful eye,
then tests its power on an apple,
slicing it neatly in halves, and tempted,
takes one half in one firm bite.

Good fruit

I miss the busy old women
searching for fruit at the A&P,
digging deep for ripeness.
They were relentless in their search,
ruthless, ruling the shelves and bins,
tossing the rejects like spent teeth.
They touched everything! All the orbs!
Squeezing, sniffing, cupping a peach
like a pitcher testing a new ball.
Their endless faith in juice and seed
was enough to unblind the stars
hidden within the blue within the blue.
Satisfied only with what burst
to life, their hairnets miniature
galaxies glittering with dew.
They appeared each Spring to test its worth,
then faded gently with the frost,
having gathered and jarred and stored their wealth.
They are gone long ago somewhere
now, perhaps caressing planets
round and smooth and good enough to eat.

Wishes on a sixtieth birthday

Apparel my mind
so it may meet and equal
the body's creeping indignities.
A mind like a whirring propeller—
that can travel back and forth in time
while remaining still.
Send me a wild wind
to keep me walking straight,
and sting my eyes to visions.
Keep wonder ever before me,
like a free, untamable horse,
turning each way I turn.
Let me still be distracted
by wind-blown hair,
or a glance to silence a sermon.
Teach me generosity
that should come with accepted age,
and freely shares the bitter-earned.
Keep the center held for now,
but never let me fear a widening ring
that guides new love to fullness.
Grant me one more harvest,
to sow my hungry thoughts,
and plant imagination deep below.

Cat without ears

One night walking I thought alone,
a part of a shadow stepped forth,
and there was a cat the size of a nightmare,
cold and black as obsidian.
Both ears gnawed off from fights,
one eye half-closed, strangely sly.
Without ears, he can hear the silence.
Nearly blind, he sees all of me.
He does not fear the darkness.
He sees through—no—sees *with* it.
And like the moon, he seems to follow
the ghost of someone lost long ago.
Each night I leave him offerings,
leftovers from beasts I've consumed.
We are blood brothers now,
we are both walking wounds.
He the stronger, more desperate and more pure.

The wolf as original dreamer

The earth would burst incandescent,
they said, but I was prepared
with an army of dreams and magic,
and each night a thousand stars
descended from the ceiling like cobalt spiders
to weave my bed of innocence.
The fall came when my father placed a book
of Peter and the Wolf before the mirror.
I could not stop watching the wolf,
its lava eyes spilling rage and violation,
teeth swirling in a snarl of white death,
its feet clawing for the earth to return.
Above, Peter clung to the tree branch
faceless, like all sadists,
tightening the noose around its tail
to suspend it through eternity,
and to make the torture exquisite,
he made music from its misery.
Tonight, alone in bed,
my wife dead, son grown and gone,
the wolf leaps from a shadow in my dream,
folds itself around me, shredded tail bleeding.
I sing gently to it,
sharing the hunger still hovering in the air.

Exodus of angels

In the store window
the old woman's hands
quivering expectations,
take down the glass angels
some once dreamed crystalline.
In their place, toys appear:
wooden horse, red racing car,
sumptuous clown, a baseball dreaming
of diamonds in the dirt, and two smooth
marbles awaiting their circle of joy.
How those angels once glittered the air!
They dazzled the bicep-sun.
Their denominations seemed everywhere
but here, now, where in this old widow's window,
they descend like the day's last longing,
as if the earth were a book re-telling itself
and forming a new conclusion.
The angels gave their hearts to glass and silence.
Now, as they depart, they leave no shadows
to wonder at the empty air,
their austere coherence replaced
with things motley, maculate,
and filled with vibrant belonging.
While the old angels, packed in straw,
are as exiled and homeless as the gods
lined dozing in a dusty museum.
The toys seem dreamed here by the night,
 a night breathlessly un-angeled,
night inhabited with laughter
and distant footsteps, with leaves
blown by stars in xylophones of dance.

Angel seeds

The Cottonwood tree sets free its angels,
its seeds that swirl like stray thoughts
in the wind's memory, astonish the light,
involve the sun, and bind us to beginnings.
They come in white shrouds over the town.
They seem to sleepwalk through the air.
They come like stars seeking new worlds.
They come to become themselves.
Some blanket the cars, some sway the winds.
Some blow in questions to the moon.
Some land in graveyards which yield and forgive.
They blow where the silence leads them.
They burst through the gaping doors of the grocery,
whispering alien voices down the aisles,
tempting the shoppers with their Winter in Spring,
to their land where all hunger ends.
Outside, in the gardens, they seek their
second life, whirling, yearning to cling deep
where stillness and darkness answer their search,
and heaven, rooted, ripens into earth.

Kyrie Eleison

My doubts have fears, my fears full reign,
so cast my love to find you in a song,
or let your arrow find my target heart.
I ask no miracle. A moon will do,
to teach me how to pray within its silence,
or guide me to a blessing in the weeds.
Chameleon my eyes to embrace your days,
or show me your palace of stars,
so I may be a peasant of your light.
Forgive my despair—it arrives unseen.
Guide my prodigal madness to a calm,
and bind me to the marrow of your love.
Come and break my heart and I'll be free.

The thrill of the transient

The fleeting know time—
near as a whispered wish,
lost as a summer of dreams.
Let it be fleeting,
the electric trill of the cicada,
the firefly engoldening and gone.
Let it be random,
the windowpaneblue
bursting with sudden angels.
Elected by grace or chance,
a heaven will not be held.
Let it live and die together—
Your midnight passion stars
or meteors that burn to longing
then plunge into the mystery.
The night accepts all comers.
Surrender to joy that thrives
at the far end of somewhere,
as the moon ripens into light,
then hides her faces gently,
one, by one, by one…

Ode to November

Ah, January!
The end of everything again.
Christmas, for example,
Christmas trees discarded
like defunct saviors, oh sighs.
Every last glance and chance
gone. Two-faced bastard.
You just don't give one damn.
All praise November!
Stuck between here and eternity,
your toothless mouth frozen in grimace,
month whose clouds stick out their
blahs, month whose leaves must
let go the Fall to Winter's
sparkling shark tooth air, knowing
each flight a rumor in the wind.
November comes for no one's sake,
carves light harsh and clear,
and keeps a mere enough of death
to keep us awake and near.

Icicle in the sun

I wish to become
such an angel of ice,
growing through loss,
tears planting Spring,
blessing and mocking
gravity, following the ghost
of my ascent
to the sun hung high
in the invisible
forever to be.

Stepping through time in Dome's Peanut Shop

There is much to praise
in a heaven for pigeons
and poets who like to wander
and wonder in circles,
and Dome's Peanuts has its own
ars poetica, seeks no explanations,
simply assumes its steamed window
purity, knows to abide the chaos
of the city, Christmas bulbs enlightened,
circling the square and the building's
hypotenuse, allows for a certain
randomness of broken shells and memories,
the trembling scent of roasted cashews
and thirsting salt, look back, I look
back because the past is ever stubborn,
wants what it wants, switches times and
locations, or dons a mask to guide us
to hidden worlds.
All we can know is memory of dreams,
dreams of memory. But I snag this sack
of nuts, clutch it to my heart and brace
the cold. And now the snow is shattered
blue and green devils, the town a grace
of swaying stoplights, it is all a heaven
paved with peanut shells. What kingdom
of nuts might I plant come Spring?
I whistle the wind's song, open the door

of the Sigma Theater, and descend
to all its secret lives, where the past
can remain forever without a ticket,
and the light is a sun-blinded angel.

Synchronicity in several colors

A propeller in a desert
imagines flight. Why not?
I spend some days just guessing at the wings,
the moon a blooming emblem of the dark,
or a lost star's last filament of heaven.
A carillon butterfly lands
on a child's toy blue ball,
balancing two worlds in one.
If two wings can touch the timeless,
my mind might heal from loss.
Time can be a lilting into flight,
a dance of color in the countless air,
or an old wet leaf in a sudden wind,
trying to return home, or a string of leaves
counting centuries back to origins.
Sometimes it coheres—so suddenly—
although it rarely lasts beyond a breath.
How can they ever end,
these half-imagined patterns in the stars?
I follow where echoes hear the strings.

Please provide a brief bio in third person with your submission

Windsong
sent to the heart's
rending,
reading loss
in the wordseed
until he learned
to speak against
the executioner, that
moon—drawn
night ghost
of ashes.

Listening
in his bones
at last he became
the prayer of the fallen
and alone.
In brief,
he became they.

Words and memory

Words
reimagined
against loss,
against the empty echo,
go through
the traumatized
silence
to a seashell,
a shelter against the cold,
against the ocean howl
that would cry us into dust.
Free, for now,
safe, for now,
to remember without pain or fear.
I remember, long ago,
how the light would enfold us,
the moon let us in,
the seeds, whisper.

My mother's voice in whispers

I hear sometimes late at night
my mother's voice inside my own,
holding, caressing it,
and hear her mother's voice
releasing their voices through me.
I only hear it when I whisper,
that voice of mother and daughter woven,
comes through my blood, my breath,
comes singing from the silence,
comes waiting for me to be.
Suddenly, one voice becomes us all,
and teaches me what I thought I knew,
brings me memories
I did not know I had forgotten.
Now my words are never mine alone.
How many mothers, how many others
await me each night in whispers?
When ill seasons come, and dreams fall away,
I'll promise to wait until they call me
to their long and longing journey home.

My grandmother's antique store in the country

came to life
each morning, glass by
glass alighting

gold watches
sharing
their pocket wealth

spinning wheel
a stillness
of breath

All sorrow
seemed
to find emptiness

Tappan stove
awaiting
fire

rows of clocks,
each hand frozen
at one number

Two Cherokee
gourds
and a flintlock

still,
at night

obsidian rings
achieved
the invisible

watch crystals
mirroring
the stars

clay marbles
in circles
cool as moons

One encyclopedia,
On the binding:
"Amen to Artillery"

And though I felt tomorrow
come wounding into time,
all night that store shone
like a jewel in a black velvet glove.

The Yo-Yo Man

The Yo-Yo Man
outside Newberry's Dime Store
conjures the light to rainbows.
He strings the spider down
a netting fine as distant stars,
spinning a balanced vertigo.
He whirls his worlds round,
makes them dance in mid-air,
sparkling for words to contain them.
And then he is gone
between now and then,
orbiting my memory like a moon.

Five and Dime

When I died,
I followed a light up the stairs
of an old rusty escalator
headed to heaven in a five and dime.
Angels were mannequins,
greeting me on other levels, other lives,
and though the escalator creaked and groaned,
I had finally come in from the cold.
I passed shelf after shelf of savings:
a spool of string, a stopped clock,
affordable toys, crutches hung on a wall,
sensible shoes, fit for a daily heaven.
The floors were run by street bums,
children, waitresses, clerks, and the poor,
who at last had food, and in a cracked window,
a spider wove a galaxy of Saturdays.
Those lazy, metal steps feared no death,
for this is a chain of perpetual motion,
returning us ever to a world
we have finally learned to see.
For everything here hums with belonging,
aisle after aisle of everyday visions,
rising free of time and gravity
in the five and dime store of eternity.

www.ingramcontent.com/pod-product-compliance
Lightning Source LLC
LaVergne TN
LVHW051501170726
843492LV00002B/754